WINTER SOLSTICE

WINTER SOLSTICE

A Memoir in Poetry

DIANA HOWARD

atmosphere press

ACKNOWLEDGEMENTS

The poem *Winter Solstice* appeared in the 2012 *Pasque Petals*, Journal of the South Dakota State Poetry Society. It was also a contest winner, sponsored by SDSPS.

TABLE OF CONTENTS

MEMORY

writing our story,
continually searching for pieces that fit.
Like a beating heart,
its existence is taken for granted,
ignored until it no longer functions.
It is as driven as the blood that winds
through our veins.
It is as fragile as our last breath.
Memory, remembered or forgotten, lives on
borrowed time.

I.

"Diana, I remember the important things"
2007

Her house rests quietly in the corner of an aged brick
    cul de sac.
It is ordinary, unassuming.
What distinguishes it as out of the ordinary, for a criminal
    that is,
is that an old woman lives there.
A woman who is kind, forgiving and a little forgetful.
A woman who can't quite tell anymore
what is true and what is false.
A woman who gives more than she takes.
For eight years, he has kept her company,
    taken her money.
She won't press charges – can't press charges
because she feels complicit.
She isn't the only one who feels that way.
We help her move. She never speaks of him again.

GOING HOME

to a landscape overgrown
with ivy and flowering ajuga,
English novels and Italian sheet music,
scattered crumbs, old coffee stains,
pieces of last night's or last week's meal,
her unwillingness to shed light
on her surroundings.

An aroma of cat is thick
in the upstairs air.

A cleaning took place
not long before my arrival.
It appeared to be only a dusting off,
a sweeping around, not moving anything
kind of cleaning that does not address

the aroma of cat
thick in the upstairs air.

I long to spring lightly
like that cat who silently
scampers by me
two steps at a time.

In my mother's home
I cannot feel light on my feet.

TAKING REFUGE

There is snow on the way.

Placid geese once again
set a harried course toward
the graying sky. They aren't fooled
by this late January thaw.

The lazy sun warms
the cold pavement, as the chilling
bite disappears from the air.
How flirtatious, this hint of spring.

Yet there is a storm brewing
and the geese know it.
You can't lull a goose into a false sense of complacency.
You won't see it trying to outguess a fickle wind.

A goose's refuge lies hidden
in a stand of prairie grass
where it curls inward, tucking its head
under its mate's down feathers.

MOTHER

seems not ready
to lay down her arms.
She may never be ready
to give up faith
that her world is still of her own making.
Yet how can she --
how can we
keep looking for silver linings
when even the hawk
has lost its way.

It appeared at my feeder
seeming unsure of how to use
the primal power in its talons.
I knew something had changed when
a chickadee began feeding
just beneath its roost,
a chickadee that
will lower its body temperature
on the earth's coldest days
to preserve its ability to fly and to sing.

Mother is the chickadee.
Mother is the hawk
and still matriarch of all.

II.

"Diana, I want you to take care of me like I took care of my mother." 2008

Diagnosis – Middle Stage Dementia

Her music will be the last thing to go because it is what she
    knows best.
They say she will lose pieces of herself and forget how to
    connect with others.
They say she will feel confused and bounce between the
    present and the past,
that she will cling to a picture, a word or a touch,
that people might take advantage of her.
They say not to argue with her, correct her or judge her.
She can't help it, they say.

What they don't say is how to answer her questions like:
What happened to all my music?
Where is my car?
When can I go home?

THE GOLD PACKAGE

sounds like a great idea.
It costs more, yet she does
need more help with medicines
more help with dressing
more help with bathing
because being old doesn't mean
naked or dirty or smelling, right?
Yet no matter how they try,
she won't let them help her.
I am torn between understanding
their frustration and admiring her resolution.

NOTES TO SELF

Address the car situation:
the running of a red light
the turning into an oncoming lane.
Impress strongly upon her that, as her passenger
I cannot know what she is going to do before she
does it.

Take car keys away.

Make signs to remind her how to:
take her medicine
take a shower
pay her bills
feed her cat
work the television
take her room key with her
dial the telephone
look at the clock

Remind her to look at the signs.

Take the signs down.

Learn how to grieve.
remind myself that everyone's grief is different.
remind myself that everyone's grief is the same.

Listen to the sound of her voice in my head.

Tears are good.

LOOKING FOR DIGNITY

She enters the dining room
cloaked in cautiousness,
looking for a familiar face or landmark.
Her road, made up of speckled
grey carpeting and carved maple handrails,
only leads her back to where she started.
These are my friends she says as we
join an almost full table.
You are lucky I say as we take our seats
between a walker and a wheelchair.
There are worse things than getting old she quips,
scanning the night's dinner menu,
afraid to admit she is lost.
She leans toward me and whispers,
I'll have what you're having.

ASSISTED LIVING

The staff told her no,
that the man from upstairs was off limits,
that being with him in an intimate way
or even just their hands entwined
under the table at dinner
needed to stop.
"They don't allow secrets here, Mom."
"I love him," she says.
"What do you love?" I ask.
"He kissed me," she says in a voice
that betrays her innocence.
After 25 years, a kiss can open
the most closeted heart.
"He's married, Mom."
Tears well in her eyes.
I could tell it didn't matter.
"Wasn't I married?" she asks.
"Yes, Mom, for forty years."
There were the tears again,
revealing a palpable loss.
She didn't need any assistance
with remembering what it felt like
to matter to someone.

DANGLING CONVERSATION

We used to talk politics,
books we were reading,

the lives of people we knew.
She was the one who told me

I didn't write well,
that my words

seemed to fade off the page
as if written in a fog.

Now, she holds
my poetry in her arms.

We would mostly agree,
except when we would not,

then she would say, reluctantly,
"I suppose so."

I wished she wouldn't have
conceded so quickly.

She wished I didn't always
need to be right.

I have grown in the art of making conversation.
She has forgotten how.

MAKING BEDS

I was taught early
how to square corners,
tuck in sides,
punch then smooth pillows.
Never leave a bed unmade.

I am 19, home for the summer
snuggled down under sheets
that smell like bleach.
I am drenched in a Boone's Farm hangover.
My mother's voice, trilling like a lark,
seeps upward through the porous oak floors.
There is the fragrant scent
of lilacs on my nightstand.
She remembered.

I am 35, in my daughter's bedroom
watching her jump on her unmade bed.
She nuzzles her face into white unicorns
on her comforter, bouncing, laughing,
falling against the wall and then onto the floor,
climbing back up and doing it all again.
I watch her playful reflection
in the mirror over her dresser yet
catch sight of something else ...
my mother standing behind me.
Her mother, a formidable shadow, stands behind her.
I climb up on my daughter's bed and jump.

I am 63. Now, we both struggle with forgetting.
My mother's perfectly made bed smells like urine.
She has hidden under it,
a half-eaten sandwich
her room key
a familiar book of poems.

I sit down next to her
open the book
to a turned down corner,
and begin to read.

WINTER SOLSTICE

There is clarity for me
on this first day of yet another winter,
as I have learned from winters past.

I watch a doe scrape frozen ground
searching for what she remembers,
her coat thick, gray, and heavy

with the task of survival
still I can see to the river and beyond.
Winter does this for me

with its absence of color,
its thinning of branches and leaves.
It has taught me to look a little closer

at a ground stripped bare,
at trees flailing in the winter wind,
to embrace the hope that lies beneath.

LOSING MEMORY

is a fierce blizzard.
Blinding snow fools
a weary traveler
down an unfamiliar road.
Like scattered diamonds, frost gathers.
Fallen leaves and prairie grass seeds
lift into the air as bitter winds
wipe the sidewalk clean.

III.

"Diana, I think I will stay here ... it is a nice place, don't you think?" 2015

As I push her wheelchair along the cement path, she seems anxious, as if each crack in the sidewalk is a threat. She hasn't spoken to me for hours except to ask where her daughter is.

We stop to feel the breeze and watch the river wandering around rocks at the bottom of the hill. She turns her face toward me, puts her hand on mine and says,

"I don't want to live like this anymore."

The thing about clogged synapses – sometimes they clear and words sneak through.

I hug her and whisper, "I know."

GIVE HER A STUFFED ANIMAL THEY SAID ...

Cat came in a box.

She wondered who would have
done such a thing.

"Who put you in there with
no food or water?" she says aloud.

She points to the piles of graying
snow outside her window.

"You must stay inside
with me," she says, wondering

just for a moment
why Cat doesn't move.

Cat lies on her lap while
she eats her soup.

The others at the table
comment on Cat's startled look,

his calm demeanor.
"He came in a box," she says.

Who says cats are not allowed
in her small-tiled room?

Cat sleeps beside her.
his paw hugging her shoulder.

Cat guards the privacy of her shower.
Cat likes to be held.

She can't bear the thought
of Cat being abandoned

of Cat having no one
to hold him or stroke him

or feed him. She weeps
when she thinks of abandonment.

TRAIN WRECK

He caught the westbound train headed
to the city in search of hope
that his tumor was smaller, his future
brighter, his deflated faith, renewed.

Hours later, his gait measured,
his head tilted tiredly to the right,
he boarded the eastbound train,
taking the seat next to mine.

As we talked I walked
head down into his worry;
his hands shook –
his words tumbled out of his mouth..

When I told him I wrote poetry,
he said he did too.
When I agreed to read it,
he asked for my address.

When I read his work, I thought
about what I had offered,
how I had misled him.
His poems talked about loss,

a guilt that pressed against his chest.
I could tell he felt abandoned.
I wanted to help him feel better
because it would help me

feel better. I didn't know
I was asking him to carry
my wounds on top of his.
I wasn't aware of my sadness.

I was traveling on a train
to visit my mother who no longer
knew me or my children.
I was steeped in grief.

He was a stranger immersed
in fear and regret,
looking for a way
to find forgiveness.

We both opened doors
we did not know how to close.

DEPARTURE

leaves me
thick with grief.

Perhaps, over time
my tender heart will toughen.

There is no manual
for how to feel as I watch

her eyes no longer exploring
or revealing, her arms

needing placement for hugs.
She always feared she would linger

too long in a vacuum of tangled memories
that tug and taunt without warning.

If she could, she would go.
If I could, I would take her.

GHOST

He appeared, smelling of cigarettes
and Crown Royal, swirling his glass,
cubes of ice clinking, losing their shape
just as she remembered him.

Glistening amber in a 3-inch glass
had always warmed his throat,
shrinking a harshness that would
otherwise strangle.

She cried out to him,
for one more whiskey kiss,
one more bitter taste
on her parched lips.

She reached toward
his bearded cheek,
catching once again
his blue-eyed twinkle.

At last ... he had come.

My mother lost my dad when he was 65 and she was 63. She lived alone until she died at the age of 93. She would get teary if Dad was ever mentioned in conversation. Sometimes she would talk to him. Her confusion broke my heart. She had lost most memories of him yet saw him in every man she met.

ORION'S BELT

Today she feels ready
trusting the moon's shadow,
appreciating the mystery
of beginnings and endings.
When she takes to the sky,
she hopes her path will swing
toward Orion's Belt.
She doesn't expect it nor
does she think that trumpets
will sound. A gentle picking on
an old guitar would be good.
When you have looked at the stars
as notes twinkling in the sky,
as worlds yet to conquer,
as beacons guiding a troubled path,
you will want to wrap
your arms around them too.

IV.

"Thank you for coming" 2017

She is dying. She has had enough of
pills, diaper changes, the struggle to comprehend.
We hold her hand, sing to her.
She is still.

"Thank you for coming," she says
her cheek resting against my hand.
The next day her breathing slows,
stops then starts then stops.

She is at peace.

EULOGY

In my dream you had died.
It was expected that I would
eulogize you which I thought
would only happen in a dream.

I talked about your endearing smile;
about the hundreds of lives you
influenced through your teaching.
I spoke of your heart,

how it opened and closed
with a cautious randomness
I could never quite predict.
I shared with them all,

your imaginative ideas
about primal vowel sounds,
and those melodic notes,
present from birth,

always at your core,
waiting to be sung.
You were, I recalled
emphatically, a kind person.

In my dream, I deeply mourned
your passing. I woke
to an unimagined silence.

CAPE HORN

Packing a wounded heart
I travel to the end of the earth,
a Chilean archipelago
that speaks of
predator and prey
lichen and layers
granite and glacier
repetition and recession
indigenous and independent
confluence and courage
sand, silk, clay,
turbidite and oblate spheroid.
I learn not to avoid
impoverished landscapes
for appearances can deceive.
Truth will wind its way
through crevasses, bubbling
up over gathering sediment.
Packing a wounded heart
I travel to the end of the earth.
Unsheathed...
I inhale its glory.

REMEMBERING

I called it quirky when she
skipped a bill payment
lost her a car in a grocery parking lot
forgot to pick me up at the airport.

Diana, I remember the important things.

I couldn't bear the thought of her
declining like her mother did
forgetting how to sing to teach
forgetting to feed her cat.

Diana, I want you to take care of me.

I remember the morning she phoned
to tell me how she went
with a drug dealer to cash
a $2000 check at 2:00 am. the night before.

Diana, my friends said I should call you.

I was on the next available plane.
When I arrived at her house
I heard her playing the piano,
a favorite Mozart concerto.

Diana, it's so nice to see you!

It was a visit that began
a nine-year journey of goodbyes.
Mine alone because she
couldn't remember hers.

This is a nice room, don't you think?

We moved the piano with her.
We moved a small pile of music.
She played and sang.
It was all she knew to do.

*Her music will be the last thing to go because it is what she
    knows best.*

After she died, I began
to know her in a different way.
She wrote stories. Kept a journal.
Deeply loved my dad.

It's important that we use our voice, she wrote.

I found a video I made
when visiting her
a year before she died.
She was singing to me.

Do you remember the words? I asked.
I'm not sure, she said.

She tapped then slapped the arm
of her chair in time with the rhythm
humming then whistling then humming,
a part of her needing to get it right.

That's how it's done, she said.

AUTHOR'S NOTES

Thank you to the patient, kind and well-trained staff at Quinn Memory Care Center, Holy Cross Village, South Bend, Indiana.

Thank you to Hospice of South Bend, Indiana for their professional and compassionate care of my mother during her last days.

Thank you to Mom's friends and students who never forgot about her. They made contact with her and shared their love for her until the day before she died.

Thank you to my brother, Mike, my brother, Bruce and my sister, Elizabeth. Our willingness to listen to each other when making decisions regarding Mom was necessary and valuable. We all did our part to help care for her.

Oh vast, tranquil peace so deep in the evening's glow.
How weary we are of wandering ...
is this perhaps death?

Im Abendrot – Joseph Von Eichendorff

ABOUT ATMOSPHERE PRESS

Atmosphere Press is an independent, full-service publisher for excellent books in all genres and for all audiences. Learn more about what we do at atmospherepress.com.

We encourage you to check out some of Atmosphere's latest releases, which are available at Amazon.com and via order from your local bookstore:

The Unsolvable Intrigue, poetry by D.C. Stoy

Words of a Feather Hawked Together, poetry by Linda Marie Hilton

I Am Not Young And I Will Die With This Car In My Garage, poetry by Blake Z. Rong

Love, Air, poetry by Lawdenmarc Decamora

To Let Myself Go, poetry by Kimberly Olivera Lainez

less on that later, poetry by Madeline Farber

The Last Hello: 99 Odes to the Body, poetry by Joe Numbers

Granddaughter of Dust, poetry by Laura Williams

Nest of Stars, poetry by Nicole Verrone

Damaged, poetry by Crystal Wells

I Would Tell You a Secret, poetry by Hayden Dansky

Aegis of Waves, poetry by Elder Gideon

Footnotes for a New Universe, by Richard A. Jones

Streetscapes, poetry by Martin Jon Porter

Feast, poetry by Alexandra Antonopoulos

River, Run! poetry by Caitlin Jackson

Poems for the Asylum, poetry by Daniel J. Lutz

Licorice, poetry by Liz Bruno

Etching the Ghost, poetry by Cathleen Cohen

Spindrift, poetry by Laurence W. Thomas

A Glorious Poetic Rage, poetry by Elmo Shade

Numbered Like the Psalms, poetry by Catharine Phillips

ABOUT THE AUTHOR

Diana Howard is a poet and children's author living along the Missouri River in southeastern South Dakota. She has published two children's books, *Applesauce* and *Boo Boo La Roo*. Her poetry has appeared in several journals and on several websites. She is a member of the South Dakota State Poetry Society and the Poetry Alliance of southwest Florida. She is inspired by those who tell her she has a "way with words."